BODY TECTONIC

Emily Abdeni-Holman is a British-Lebanese writer. She grew up in Warlingham (UK) and Jamhour (Lebanon), and worked as an arts and culture writer in Beirut before pursuing a doctorate in literature in the UK. Her first novel, *At the Pine House*, takes place in Jamhour in the 1960s-70s. She currently lives in Cambridgeshire.

Emily Abdeni-Holman writes with humane clarity about the ways we embody physical, geographic and emotional states: 'how we put our body in places / where nothing happens, places for signs and wonders'. The body of which she writes is simultaneously multiple and singular as she examines bodily need in Lebanon (while inflation rises and rises), or interrogates the body-focussed wellness industry. Formally, too, her poetry is inventive: words are shared across gulfs; the conversation is picked up by other times and selves, entangled and interconnected. The stanzas of the poem become tectonic plates which collide with - and drift from - each other, finding parallels and mirrorings between cultures and voices. Bodies override others or meet in understanding, the potential for earthquakes and ruptures rumbling underneath. *Body Tectonic* is wise, urgent, and deeply resonant. As moving act of witness and finely wrought work of art, I have read nothing else quite like it.
— Penny Boxall

Abdeni-Holman's Lebanon is both violent and poignant. The poems capture the dehumanising nature of the ongoing crises engulfing a suffocating nation in freefall. Emily deftly pieces together headlines, testimonies, anecdotes and reports in order to tell the story of a devastating economic collapse, physical and mental carnage, power cuts, fuel shortages, migration and a pervasive sense of loss. *Body Tectonic*, to roughly translate a Lebanese expression, has its finger firmly 'in the wound' and refuses to let go.
— Naji Bakhti

Body Tectonic presents an unsettling poetry of witness and open-ended inquiry into the lived experience of Lebanon's troubled recent history. The body – both physical and politic – becomes the focus of social, material and economic crisis, as a site of shock, loss and suffering, but also 'resilience' – a word interrogated with sensitivity throughout the book. This in turn leads, implicitly, to what is at stake for the soul – the inner life, no less actual for its bafflement in the face of onrushing circumstances – and the source of what (if anything) lives, and what carries on, despite disaster. Combining reportage and contemplation in its inventive use of language, organising its sense through ruptured syntax, this humane and intelligent work examines at first hand matters laid within our history that 'cannot be undone' – and the ways in which, in the face of crisis, the human body 'knows all over again what's real'.
— Gregory Leadbetter

Body Tectonic is an extraordinary poetic narrative. Emily Abdeni-Holman charts the disintegration of a seemingly stable society, showing how the underlying fault lines resurface in the face of a major incident that the west took an interest in for perhaps a week, and has probably now forgotten. A timely reminder that we are only a careless act away from a cascade of consequences that can undermine a whole country, no matter how sophisticated it might seem on the surface.
— Cherry Potts

Body Tectonic

Emily Abdeni-Holman

Broken Sleep Books

NOTE: All statistics, data, and quotations (given in italics) are from news coverage or firsthand testimonies.

© 2024, Emily Abdeni-Holman. All rights reserved; no part of this book may be reproduced by any means without the publisher's permission.

ISBN: 978-1-916938-30-4

The author has asserted their right to be identified as the author of this Work in accordance with the Copyright, Designs and Patents Act 1988

Cover designed by Stuart McPherson

Edited by Kit Ingram

Typeset by Aaron Kent

Broken Sleep Books Ltd
PO BOX 102
Llandysul
SA44 9BG

CONTENTS

If this is a body 9

Body Tectonic 10

Notes on Arabic words 113

*For all those living in precarity,
and for the stability of the lands they long for.*

IF THIS IS A BODY

Which is the name, after all, for a person who is dead
a word used in opposition to *mind* and *soul*
has feelings to regulate instead of heed
is treated as the source of the trouble
is a little tense right now
requires food, drink, and washing in emergency
requires tenderness in emergency
requires these things especially in emergency
bears marks bearing our living
cannot be undone

1. Sleep, work, bed, he is saying, standing in the heat
   on the turn of the winding path where we run, standing
   with a woman whose hands pat her hijab as she listens,
   offering to it what she cannot give him, as he tells
   what each day holds now, sleep, work, bed: nom, cheghel, takhet,
   as if sleep and bed are different states (and they are),
   one what comes eventually, one the place we go to wait
   till it does, sweating humid on July nights, in an electricless
   Lebanon: neither fans nor AC, bed an interminable site
   of waiting to see whether sleep will come before tomorrow,
   breathing into fug's thick warmth, body wearing ways
   it would never have chosen when, as a child, it dreamt
   of what would come, sleep, work, bed, in a stateless
   Lebanon, where mercy is how eventually bed turns to sleep

2. sleep, work, bed: yes, how we put our body in places
where nothing happens, places for signs and wonders,
and nothing happens, only echoes and waiting, what
passes is only time, what grows is weariness and age,
what goes on is endurance; and the things place is made for
are wistful dreams, growing quieter, growing harsher,
more crude and grasping, crave of sleep, darkening
hunger, frantic sex frustrated for release, body wasting
while it waits and hope concatenating into urgent fantasies
to hide shamefully in the morning: I go to bed to wait
for sleep, he is not saying, sleep does not come, only
onslaught and worry, he is not saying, and she listens,
thinking — imagine it — how bodies & places & happenings
are meant to meet and how, when they do not, we drift, a fluke

3.   fluke in the light, drifting, she might be thinking,
or how a life passes waiting for things to resolve
themselves, waiting for real life to begin, or living
(as she has heard him say) on the edge of real life
knowing this is it   & now he is saying yesterday
for four hours he was queueing on a highway waiting
for petrol, and he had more luck than his neighbour
who slept there in his car overnight   even the rich,
he is saying, even those with a backlog of cash-crisp
savings or supply of dollars fresh enough to hold value
are having to queue and so they pay someone with time
on his hands   (so many workless men)   time enough
to sit in the car   (so many workless men)   inch forward
schwe schwe by the hour   it's a job as good as another

4. another thing, he is saying — and perhaps it's because he is
sleepless (though not yet bedless) that he says these things:
we all know what a night without sleep or with not enough
can do to the body — another thing is that anyway when
you get to the front of the queue they only top you up
with half what you need, half or quarter of a tank, unless
you slip across a little extra, or if you're a beautiful woman
and the guy holding the pump is in the mood to relax
his frowning forehead and empty his ears for a moment
of all honks & shouts & yallas and forget for a moment
what a shitty morning it's been and the fact each person
in each car is blaming him (he does, after all, bear the pump,
& he does at times, it's true, send gas surging longer): well, then he might
take handhot notes   inhale sweet-faced smile   push finger down

5. down the highway this morning, she announces, on
right down the highway, the cars extended for maybe
a kilometre down the highway, maybe more, and they're
not moving, the fuel-line just gets longer but the cars
hardly move, even when they get their quota and go on —
it's like this, like it's a permanent sculpture on the highway,
even when the pieces change — it's an ongoing fixture now,
and already I can't remember what it's like to see a highway
clogged only with traffic, the gas-station a place you go
for a break   not a sculpture, he says, I think of it like
a snakeskin, a vacant shell   and did you hear, she says,
last month a woman was out searching, she and four daughters
searching for fuel to get her husband from the airport
an army vehicle hit them and they died

6. died is not accurate, she thinks later, I should've said
were killed, who cares it wasn't intentional and yes
it was a terrible accident, but what is the word or is there
a word for accidents that shouldn't happen, materialising
not from bad luck or bad timing or clumsiness or stupidity
(and these hurt enough)   what's the name for accident
caused by colliding circumstances caused by deliberate neglect,
or structural culpability, or complicity so brazen and vast
that *complicity*, in fact, yes so it turns out, is a very real
very stark malevolence governing this way of the world
we've strung ourselves to   what is the name for accident
like that, because these are what occur now   blastfire
ammonium nitrate   fuel tanker explosion   circumstances
not inevitable, not random   which could've been averted

7. averted eyes are not what we see here, not in Lebanon
over these days during this summer, when everyone
knows everyone else is struggling, even the ones
struggling less than you   and that is why
this conversation between the man and the woman
touches passersby who happen to hear a snatch of phrase,
the kind of conversation (fearful & shameful & sad)
usually kept for indoor nights and alcohol, not a morning
on a jogging-route where all day long people arrive
for their daily stroll and greet each other and even wait
for each other so they can walk together   often
this country has been a place where litter on streets
is sped rolling past in a window-shut jeep   but
every day now sees us look out for each other and listen

8. listen to your body, people rich in countries say,
people safe in countries   *listen to what you need*
rich, safe, secure   rich means built on solid ground
it means the land beneath you is stable   it means
the body you are   has something to say other than
make me well   it means it will take   an awful
lot   to make the ground shift beneath your feet
    like tectonic plates, tired of the old   searching
for cavities fresh and new   to fit themselves into
or else it will take   very little to piss you off
or disturb you   because the uneven nook   in your
quiet cranny   could've been fashioned better
& like the princess atop a mattress atop a pea   you'll
find your body   is in danger of not being comfortable

9. comfortable   here we don't remind ourselves
   to listen to our body   here our body is telling us
   all day and night   our body says things are wrong here
          all day and night we know it   all day and night
   the ground our feet are standing on   is apt to tremble
   yes, apt to tickle and toss   apt to teeter, totter, tingle
   apt to tear, apt to turn, apt to trample onto us   apt to rise up
   and take over, apt to overwhelm, apt to do what ground
   should not   go where ground   does not   and so
         each time we walk   we   find
            we go gingerly   even when we run
   to each other, even when we dance, each time we sit & share
   a drink   giggling, drifting, tripping, dozing   our body
   knows   even though   all the while   our minds forgot

10. — forgot about this: did you know days before the first lockdown in England someone ran into the supermarket shouting we're all gonna die (it was in iceland it was before queues for shops began) everyone crowding stocking and one woman shouting we're all gonna die, we're all gonna die, woman in her fifties kids laughing & fear inside cold then rules came & body adjusted body politic and body social body going along with not being near no other body not seeing new things learning more ways to get comfortable slack clothes, tv, isolated fragments of lives ongoing hidden enclosed & not being known and a year later the UK had a petrol crisis and the shock was queues for fuel could happen in Britain, where things reliably go on —

11. on things go in Lebanon without there being change
not state not structure not system network programme
template model tendency   everyone wants to believe
the best, even while seeing what there is   we want to hope
we trust things will improve   every so often one of us says
they shouldn't have been so resilient   we're talking
about our parents' generation, who went on   in war
and went on in another war and went on some more
when things went on being hard went on costing more
who went on when their passport went suspicious
to many countries went on raising children building
homes warming water connecting gas generating
electricity learning-teaching languages-maths-dance
smoke-lining eyes skimming noses driving fast

12. fast as a raqwe cascades over when it boils
chemicals exploded glass shattered heights dashed
and blood crashed blood billowed blood spat skin
and the country stopped while on screen it shook
call after call sent networks down & those who could
went home & those who could stopped to help
& those at home waited and waited and waited-in-hope
(the curious hope that holds up dread, says, God: look,
look God don't do any of this — I've thought it through
— I've thought it like a protection to stop you)
      on every street, every alley, all along the road
there was plenty of help   there was the help
disaster makes when everything is blown away   body
knows all over again what's real body remembers   rushes to help

13. help like you help when you love a child
    and they open their mouth to yawl and there's
    a split second before the face-split emits sound
    and there's a split second before ears split
    with sound and in that split of time & soundless face
    the care to stop them being sad   help them
    while they're sad   love them so they'll
    never be sad   body leaps to lift them
    heart to chest   soften them with breath
    gentle warm head breast   body leaps to hold
    womb raw child   body leaps to help
    and the body that's been used to being its own
    remembers what it is not to be alone   body
    remembers another kind of real   rushes to help

14. help is what you expect from a man in charge
    man running a country, head of state, wearing a suit
    smart balding head   gentle glasses   smiling as he passes
    pausing often enough to tell you he *thinks*
    (thinks and will not be rushed)   every so often
    announcing brilliance with an announcement prior
    to warn you brilliance is coming, certainly tomorrow,
    tweets brilliance and then retweets it and likes
    others retweeting it too   & here we have many men
    clamouring to be in charge   and they tell you
    how they love your country   and they tell you
    it deserves better and they won't do it again   won't
    let it happen again   nothing like this will happen
    on my watch   (and if it does)   not   ever   again

15. again and again, same things happening, on and on
through years and decades   and the question now
is whether the country has a character and a memory
and so keeps insisting on itself when something
comes up (threatens) differently   & the question
now is what is this land's personality that keeps on
reclaiming itself restating itself insisting on itself
    & the question now   is whether personality
is instead a concoction, something growing itself
into being   a kind of protection   self-thickening skin
    warfightdeathcorruption
rapeshootsteal   like a person sitting inside
for years on end   sitting inside   warfightdeath
corruption   sitting inside   letting no one in

16. in September a cabinet forms   first time
    in more than a year   August saw a fuel tanker
    explode   saw a hospital release a statement:
    soon we will not have enough electricity
    to give dialysis or sustain life-support, and so
    approximately 40 adults 15 children will die imminently
    and a further 180 within a few days
        August saw taxis treble-quadruple their prices
    then stop running for the cost of fuel & night-long queue
    to get it   August saw supermarket delivery stop
    saw all kinds of delivery stop   saw elderly isolated infirm
    helped fresh every few days by neighbours family friends
    saw kindness and openness and no government help
    saw a thirty-four-year-old become a father   first time

17. time continuing in an electricless Lebanon   time
continuing everywhere   and how ordinary it is
when time continues where states are failing and things
that run come to a stop   & time goes on and kids
are born into moneyless supportless jobless families
and kids are born into the hope and love kids bear
    the new father has no way to heat his home
fuel price mushrooming   40,000 for twenty litres
67,000 for twenty litres   200,000 for twenty litres
fuel needed for cars, for generators   the state provides
(inshallah) two hours electricity a day   other hours
powerless or dependent on generators dependent on fuel
200,000 twenty litres   200,000 was over $100
now it costs the same but equals ten   salaries unchanged

18. unchanged changed   hard to mark the meaning of change
    while everything is static and in flux   & those who can
    are going where they can   Dubai Saudi France Jordan
    Kuwait Qatar Canada Mexico Australia Brazil the USA
    those who can are fleeing   those who can (take note)
    are doctors university professors medical professionals
    the multilingual   the better-off   the young
    those who can't   and some who won't   stay
        the August-born child is from a mountain region
    mountain whose trees are ancient   ancient mountain trees
    of ancient Lebanon   the local economy relied on apple exports
    the local economy has crashed   there is no money
    for fuel for electricity for homes for hospitals for work
    no money for heating   so ancient mountain trees are burnt

19. burnt bright fire heat   *eventually* (the mayor says)
    eventually an environmental NGO, the Lebanese state,
    or another country   will take care of the people,
    give them fuel at a reasonable price   I tell people this
    even if I don't believe it myself, tell them to be patient
    eventually help hope change has to come   even if I don't
    believe it myself   has to   even if   has to
        even if   myself I don't believe   when is faith
    a failure of responsibility   when is it what creates change
    simply by going on   it's not that a body gets used to anything
        it's that they (we) go on, it's all they (we) can do
    kids still need raising in war   has to   even if   has to
    the father of the newborn works for the municipality
    he is selling his cellphone so he doesn't start to burn trees

20. trees mark Lebanon from the beginning: the earliest
    references speak of the cedar   Hiram of Tyre who sends
    cedar wood to Solomon for his temple   cedars of Lebanon
    enduring strong emblazoned across the land   mountains
    of Lebanon covered in cedars pine gorse thistle cypresses firs
    forests of Lebanon with scorpions under stones and caves under
    soil and caverns of rock under water and salt-fresh fish flickering
    in water and snow-covered mountains and sparse bare winter-bright
    grottos in the mountains where womenmen pray under the moon
    faces up to the stars and hands on branches fashioned into signs
    whose meanings matter less than the sake of the fashioning
    gently fervent caress of skin on something living & loved
    trees shading womenmen on hot days rainy days dark days
            days now are dark   in October state electricity cut

21. cut came back cut again back again   the patternpitpattern
    has been going on for years   for decades and more
    on again off again   stable unstable   worth a try not worth it
    stay or go or go stay go keep a foot in two places keep a family
    in many places it's a not-quite-exile — you can always go back
    (and you do) — but you can never put down your battle-wear
    cannot rely on safety from the state security from the state
    if your parents get ill or your child falls down or your cash
    falls short you will turn to your neighbour who will babysit
    or make a call   bring round moloukhiye   even say
    you can move in   like the father of the newborn
    who will live with his neighbours if he cannot pay to heat
    his home   no form to fill in or pledge to make out
    middle-class is in poverty now   middle-class is gone now

22. now (like always) they're saying it's a sectarian thing
the Maronite militia the Shia militia the sectarian system
the Taif accord the PM a Sunni the president a Christian
the speaker of parliament has to be Shia what about the Druze
what about the Orthodox eighteen sects (I heard it was seventeen)
how do they do it all at each other's throats it's only the system
keeping things safe weren't there Jews once what happened
to Lebanon's Jews don't mention Israel don't mention Jerusalem
sometimes best too not to mention Palestinians and what about
those Syrians working cheaper working for nothing working
illegally up in the Bekaa down in the camps down in the parking
of your apartment block seven kids and the parents in a room
& don't tell the building committee (they said they'll throw them out
if there's over four) good thing they're hamstrung or they might run

23. run is controversial run is contested run is thought
escape by some, wise by others: basically necessary,
basic responsibility, if you have a desire to be held
in an institution — framework — structure — system
if life makes sense to you with a sense of direction
if you have a purpose (the importance of structures)
(the littleness of what you can do against structures)
          a lot of life goes on fighting structures
at some point the fight   will   could   will
stop making sense, it will be something you no longer
can go on with   you will pack your clothes you will
pack your children's clothes you will kiss your mother
you will tell your mother, be careful, and she will tell you
don't go don't leave our land   she will tell you   I won't go

24. go on packing, put all the things of your life
    into boxes to store in this country you do not trust
    bury them deep or reinforce cardboard-cum-plastic
    pay for security from air from heat from eager hands
    store your possessions as if one day   as if you might
    one day decide to come here again & wish you had boxes
    with your own things in for unpacking   pack kids' toys
    you can't throw for the love of them   pack them to keep to gather dust
    pack those toys still favoured and mark them for the plane
    mark them for your ongoing life, instead of this old one,
    ruptured now   is life something belonging to place
    or people (somehow it goes on in both) & are you
    dislocated now, an expat, migrant, or diaspora
    exile is the truest thing you're feeling now

25. now what is happening to people's body is
    body is cold or hot or hungry   body is
    humiliated   body is spending time in ways no body
    wants to spend, waiting in half-day-queues, rifling bins
    begging from cars from hands begging with eyes &
         this is how we lose our softness, says Ta-Nehisi Coates
    the port explosion should have been a converging moment
       in a sense it was, time converged, ground shifted
    tectonic plates shifted   but since then time has only gone on
    ground shifting less dramatically and more humiliatingly
    and more despairingly for being ignored   & body
    going on enduring   not getting used to, not getting
    used to, but going on, in any case, because what else
         nom, cheghel, takhet   sleep, work, bed

26. bed, where the head of your loved one rests,
    where the body of your loved one seeps into your body,
    or where you try to trick yourself to sleep, with little light
    or none at all, or where you treat yourself because life
    is hard, and a shot of baileys or a draw on weed or a bite
    of chocolate might make rest come faster   bed
    is where it's easy now not to get caught in blue light
    because no current flows   though it's true
    electricity tends (ayre bi hazze) to come in the night
    when people can use it less   then you leap up
    to charge phones laptops UPS check fridge, wish
    you'd filled the goddamn freezer   leap up in the night
    to hoover, suck hair & dirt while kahraba is coming   October,
    where the cost of fuel has gone up to 300,000 today

27. today 300,000   not so long ago, in June, mister minister for energy said Those Who Can't Pay 200,000 For A Tank Should Stop Using A Car And Use Something Else   (many alternatives float around) (infrastructure for shared transport certainly exists)   those days seem good now   it's true the mess is no longer subsidies   mess now is inflation whose momentum will not stop, whose end is not in sight every cost is going   up   up   up
what we have in Lebanon are multiple crises collapsed in one 80% require humanitarian assistance — intervention — aid *there is a deep rift between social and political classes*
     yes, *in Lebanon, there is a perfect storm*
(there is a slow train coming, if there were trains to come)

28. come, she says, when they meet on the path again
    come with me to my house, come see my parents,
    my parents will be happy to see you   me too, I will
    be happy, I must bring something   forget it, she says,
    just come   they are neither formal now nor informal
        months since he told her he could not sleep
    months since he said life was whittled to bed-&-work
    some days (Fouad here) *some days you stick your hand
    in your pocket and find nothing   I leave the house
    and just pray   whatever I make, it does nothing, it's a joke*
        for a moment he is silent as they stand
    alert to a wind of winter behind the shadowed pine-breeze
        what scares me, he tells her, is this is not a joke
    not one part of this is not true or not real   this is not a joke

29. joke would be a nice thing   would be a fine thing
    they like a joke, she and him   they send each other
    emojis of fire   one day her phone pings and it's a ship
    in water   she replies with a question mark & he
    tells her the ship is sinking   she sends a smiley face
    she does not know if it's a joke   already a month gone
    and it's true time is slow while it's going, but then she realises
    it's *more than two years* since crisis began, since inflation ran
    since revolution took a stand since   for the fifth or sixth time
    in her hopeless ardent memory   people thought, like she did,
    this was the turning-point to change   (Bassil, Yaman, Maan,
    Fouad here)   *all expressing hopes the small protests
    happening across the country   would gain momentum*
    believing in turning-points could be a foolish thing   could

30. could be beautiful   results (and it shouldn't be this way)
results are what will tell   for now only stasis
and too many shocking stories   savings dwindled
to nothing   only a certain amount can be taken out
each month, at a third, an eighth, a twentieth of its value
one man hopes to sell his kidney
hope is a thing to be adjusted   what we plan for, dream of
these are smaller now   smaller and less simple
in Lebanon (Khalil here) *no one lives off their salary*
we stay alive by incurring debt on top of our salaries
(Tammam here) *we are worse off than it ever was in the past*
we are similar to how Beirut was in 1994, 1995
hope for turning-points   could be a beautiful thing
could be foolish   *two years since this began*

31. began in October two years ago: now November winds
preface November rain, and the things the woman
thought would not happen, and the things the woman
thought would be solved by now — these are only starting
— these days are only early — and the things the woman
thought about how the future would be   these turn out
to be based on what the past has told her things are like
and she didn't understand   she doesn't understand
    time doesn't work that way   the years
to come have so little in common with the years
a life begins with   years in which you learn the world
childlike ways & childlike things form you   the years
(all years) are adult now   & all days (in the end) are early
all emerging from what went before   while also blinding

32. blinding   us   with their   strangeness   their   un
    fath   om   ability   *early days* refers to something new
    but even the unexpected has roots & comes from somewhere
        did you know in english the word *inure* means
    to toughen and also to acclimatise   it means to harden up,
    thicken-your-skin, and also to habituate   and these are
    not the same   not until you have been in a place
    where adjusting & turning   hard   cold   old
    where these go together   (if you have been there we guess
    you have been there long)   strange, how the longer we go on
    the stonier we get, accustomed to what we would not,
    in early years, like to imagine ourselves accustomed to
        so she is always expecting the worst — not in anticipation,
    not as preventative (a kind of magical thinking), but because

33. because the worst is what it makes sense to be used to
one measure of a sick society is how much suffering it can resign itself to (this in an American magazine talking of American problems)   & the question now is does this country have a character it cannot turn down turn back turn aside turn away turn from   *I believe* (Charif here) *the history of Lebanon and of the Lebanese people is a history of permanent denial   it is impossible to live in a country poisoned by corruption speculation debt without suspecting this won't all come crashing down   deep down   everyone must've suspected but we carried on regardless, because for years the country offered us an exceptional quality of life*   not easy   not easy   to know whether it makes sense to be here

34. here, says the woman to the man on the path as they walk,
not this time to her home (that was a mistake, and it would
not make sense to repeat the error the embarrassment & besides
her parents — her kind and hospitable parents, whose faces
darkened when he proffered his soiled handpicked flowers —
her parents have forbidden it)   nor is it to his home they walk
    each time he reaches home his predicament, which
he never in any case stops thinking of, even for moments,
his predicament moves through his body, or stretches
dormant bones, reminds itself of the beauty of its limbs,
his predicament revives itself and his worries become
bodily things, felt right through, and his bed   the sight of his bed
makes his eyes begin to gather water, dust, dust and water
until a dense stinging thud   which won't become tears

35. tears his gut into a tinny threading pulse, which he
has learnt to recognise, though not to identify, as despair —
     no, where they walk is nowhere particular, but
although they do not go round in visible circles, they accept
nevertheless to cross back and forth the same winding path,
up, down, forward till the end then turn and forward again,
and time passes this way, just as it would if they were in circles,
or for that matter going straight and never back on themselves
I spend my days she is saying *going back* and he does not
say his opinion, which is that back is better than not moving
nothing is worse than stagnation   even if she would grin
and say, sure, but stagnation sounds better when you call it stillness
     and he would have to grin too and agree, have to because
it's only she, these days, who makes his face move that way

36. that way isn't right, she says, as he turns at the turn
 of the path   here, follow me   I never
 noticed this route   sometimes it's good to go
 a way that's not been evident   I get it,
 but I prefer ways plainly lit, so I know not only
 what I'm facing, but also what I'm heading towards
      that would be a lie though   (the bashfulness
 she might once have had to call him a liar
 does not now cross her mind)   who can know
 where they're headed   (three months since
 she saw him & truly no space in her for any kind
 of second-guessing   call it spontaneity, it isn't
 true sincerity   it's speaking without space to stop)
       the secret way they walk is thickening with trash

37. trash won't stop their steps, trash has become
    the way of the land   all the youth (so many youth)
    have been on protests   protect the turtles
    pick up litter   clean out the river   sweep up
    the shores   save our wildlife   spread spread
    the recycling word   put food out for strays
    better yet give them homes   clear up our streets
         once   we were driving down the highway
    driving south to Beirut from Byblos, singing to make
    our voices heard in other cars   we saw a hand
         drop a bottle from a window ahead of us
    before the car was caught in a jam   we leapt out
    grabbed the bottle, leapt in, sped up, threw the bottle
    through the open window   mish haram!   mballa, haram

38. haram is always a frequent word, only now
    it's less an expression, more an observation
    and it hurts to say it more than it used to, hurts to see
    the flagrancy with which good laws (legal & otherwise)
    are breached   but neither walker now speaks haram
    to see the mounting way broken with glass, cigarettes,
    plastic coffee cups, mana'eesh paper, olive stones, shells
    of nuts and seeds, something dead neither of them can see,
    whose smell neither of them mentions, mad amounts
    of orange peel   (clementines are in season now, when
    a couple of hours after lunch — newly a source of trouble,
    this halfway-through-the-day-meal — day will be dark & damp)
           the trashy way leads them up the hill, as if trash
    has no interest in gravity or tumbling, but settles in where it falls

39. falls and rises, she can tell, his heartbeat changing tacks
    to cope along this upward way   she imagines him
    a little embarrassed to find it harder going than she does
    it's gratifying, but after all, she knows the way, and (as he says)
    knowledge of what is coming is half the battle in facing it
       seeing the sweat of him in the cooling nightward air
    makes her feel a little harsher, but she was already on her way
    to harshness, and somehow when she sees him look so tired
    impatience kindles, and the words she might have used
    to console him seem empty of purpose   and she cannot
    muster tongue to phrases her mind has said to him
    before his body was here   they go up, up, up, in silence
    sometimes it's good, to see something different   quiet
    only she doesn't any longer know why she chose this way

40. this way or that way or what way to go on
is a topic on many minds these days
(Rayan here) *there is never any sense of urgency to help people*
(Firass here) *it's very difficult to tell hospitals to not ask
patients to pay extra   I'm not just saying this to scare people
but I really think the system is on the brink*
(Yukie here) *a lot of women are looking for infant formula
families cannot afford*   more than half the people surveyed
(reports a newspaper) say they experience *great sadness*
more than six in ten Lebanese would like to leave permanently
     great sadness   now each passing month
sees us look back for how things were a week ago, a day ago,
the before-time, before this latest-sorry-tale, as if time
is moving faster than we are and our work to play catch-up

41. catch-up! catch-up! catch-up with the news!   by the time
our body has adjusted to a vast new change
something else is replacing it (67,000, 200,000, 380,000)
    forget queues for petrol, now we queue for bread
the statistics are terrible, and it's only when we hear them
we get some sense of comprehension of what, each day,
we moved through to get to the precious point of evening
when people gather but more importantly time does, time
done for the day, everything steadying into itself
into a halt   *great sadness*   and now we are beginning
(who are we kidding) to be habituated to crisis, to be used
to operating on short-term-reactors, used, not so much
to flash-fast fast-as-flesh decision-making — probably we'll
never be good at deciding quickly — as used to conditions

42. conditions telling us decisions must be made
    with a tight head, aching stomach, pitfall heart pulsating
    partly just to tell us   you can't go on like this
    this way you're accustomed to going on   so perhaps
    it's not time that passes the same, as the conditions
    our body lives, which is in a way our younger selves
    would love to shriek *isn't living at all! is only existing!*
    perhaps it's not time dragging on so slowly till evening
    when we gather on the balcony, perhaps it's our body
    dragging to reach the witching hour, the only one
    worth the wait, gather on the balcony, two or three,
    seven, fifteen if the kids' friends stay, kids who are
    no longer kids, but seem like it, because they (we)
    have no money, even those who work   they (we) still

43. still need help to fuel the car   still don't understand
    still talk about protest & change   still suggest visas to go
    still close eyes to dream   and when evening comes
    we sit together with whisky on ice and we breathe
    knowing air tastes better with sharpness in it
    better to do things in a way where they (we) hurt
    and when our throat burns our body sighs relief
    sighs into itself   thank god day is done and it's dark
    and we have nothing to feel we ought to do, we can do
    the nothing it feels right to do, knowing nobody at this time
    can ask more   ice-cold whisky & a cigarette whose smoke
    smells of cocoa, calling to the woman at moments —
    odd spots where she finds herself outside her mind, no
    calculation, no second-guessing, no speculation or prediction

44. (prediction doesn't work, in any case, she knows now —
she's always thought thinking about things would make
some difference to them — thinking to keep harm
from taking place, imagining futures to make them real —
everything that happens she has read some meaning into
and when disaster comes, each time, she has believed
disaster will be heeded — so small her belief, not solution,
not being saved, not rescued, but recognised, yes,
she's always thought whatever happened would be seen
and, once seen, responded to — and though it seems
this is   not the case   she hasn't stopped believing it
might, one way or another, come to be true   because
believing that makes more sense than having no movement
to belief or to hope, and no trust in love, in her at all) —

45. — all there is, in these moments, is senses and longing
and the coolness of ice tanged with whisky in the throat,
which makes hope closer to the brave than to the self-deluding
side of things   in these moments, while she's holding
the cigarette (adult, smelly, scary cigarette, which
in most other countries comes with a sign saying
it will kill you faster than would otherwise be the case)
the cigarette she draws on, draws in, blessed cigarette,
adult relief for adult fears   then, the smell — when
she happens to catch it with no awareness it was coming
with no awareness for who she is and has become
or why it is she has to smoke — smell seizes her to early years,
when being tucked up safe in bed was maximum good,
when kiss goodnight smelt like cocoa, no matter who

46. who it was who gave her the kiss, kiss goodnight
    strong with cocoa, because somewhere she had heard
    or read that cocoa is what children have before sleep,
    and each night she breathed in knowing whatever
    she smelt was cocoa   and somewhere along the way
    it really did become the chocolate-smelling drink
    at some point someone bought some from abroad
    and so the night-dream-ritual became part of how she lived,
    how she was kissed, how she slept   but
    none of this works unless she is taken by surprise, and when
    she smells a cigarette her usual reaction is to ruffle
    her nose and turn away, swing the hijab as if to let a layer
    of herself linger between the thing she holds in her fingers
    and the lungs and lips she uses to draw it mightily in

47. in her case, too, sleep has suffered   as a child she slept
in ways she thinks at times might never come again
though each night sleep does come, eventually, and faster
now nights are colder   each day when she wakes
she does feel briefly refreshed   she likes to think
of a younger her, the young woman she was not so long ago
a year or two, never having heard the rote & quandary
of nom-cheghel-takhet   not so long ago she too had hopes
bursts of protests across the country would gather, spread,
take off   at least she works, it's true   *at least* not because
work equals income   (mostly it does not)   but because
colleagues & laughter & moving from one place to another
these make the day faster   until blessed time of night
when she breathes in smoke   breathes smoke in

48. in her body there's usually nothing, these days,
other than calculations, guesses, suppositions, worries
about her parents her siblings her nephews her friends
her colleagues (her future her art her inner life)
amazement at new amazing daily facts, but most of all,
most of all the fact that with all other amazing changes
— inflation long past the last measurement she heard,
211 percent, and salaries not one thousand lira
(and currency doesn't come much smaller than that)
not one thousand lira changed — with amazement is quiet
sometimes she summons the names of two babies, Yasmine,
Jouri, who hospitals turned away for lack of money lack of meds
    they died   *a little angel's life was put a price tag*
    (@ritabes here)   *instead of given emergency care*

49. care here, in the presence of her people, cared for
by those asking nothing from her, these people who've
always been there   her eyes look about and she's grateful
her mind says, thank god we are here, together, able
to eat, it's this time of day and togetherness we wait for
    only there's also the restlessness that's been coming
these last months, strong in her body   demanding
      won't let her ignore it   urging her
    and who knows for what or from where it comes
what she knows is   she isn't happy, sitting here
and this isn't a fact in itself, but a happenstance linked
to a fact   the fact she knows there is   not must be
but is   more than this way of trickling through a life,
used to the earth trickling beneath her feet, until gaps

50. gaps become larger than ground
and at the same time going on, every day, so she
barely registers the gaps growing and days passing
days going *great sadness*
we treat this (says the American magazine) as *lamentable*
mysterious, out of our control   but there are things
one shouldn't get over too quickly   and things
one should never get used to   she nods, but *should*
is not a word she wants ruling her   it's easier by far
to pronounce from without   easier by far to decide
on something in a mind   whether a body
heeds will depend on ground, air, sky, depend on things
a body is occupied with, cigarettes, cocoa, other bodies,
smelly death, steadily warming days, ready smiles, orange peel

51. peel me some loz akhdar, she says, holding them out
to him, and he laughs, to see her carrying green almonds
on their walk   we'll have to sit, he says, and she agrees,
doesn't suggest a quiet path or spot out-of-the-way
together they walk to the place-with-a-view where too many go
and they find a gap   and less slowly than anticipated
they eat their way through a kilo of fresh nuts
       and while she is looking at him she realises
although he is not thin, although to look at him nothing
is out of place   she realises he is bereft   she wonders
if he will tell her   or whether she will never know
*Lebanon is very sadly in freefall and it's quickly hitting
rock bottom*   recently a masked man held a pharmacist
at gunpoint   asking for babyfood   *great sadness*

52. sadness and anxiety coexisting with smiles, with laughter
laughter of Lebanon, living & laughing here, fingernails
thick with green almond skin, because she brought nothing
but the nuts, and so teeth and nails are having to do
the work a tool makes in a moment   it doesn't take long
    they've been doing it all their lives   she imagines
there's something in him, despite the disappointment,
that will remember this time, remember this time
and see youth in it, though they are not so young,
remember legs swinging over the view, remember
an uneven surface poking pockmarks in their backsides,
remember watching over the edge of town, over the city,
right over the extension of the city to the coast, remember
pine trees above them, almonds softening in their hands

53. hands that could, eventually, reach out to touch the other's
and might eventually one day   but not tonight
not tonight, when it's cold, when the evening's chill
calls for huddling, huddling close in, and they aren't ready,
can't be ready, she can't see that any more than she can see
the two of them meeting more than every-so-oftenly   but
she likes the thought   she's grateful the idea could come
amidst all this, and especially amidst the stolidness of her
(there is no other word)   the slow blocking up of her body
     not so blocked after all   it's quite a discovery,
this end-of-March evening, the day the clocks change,
days on their way to becoming warm, nights cool still
     although she feels torpid and stilted and stoppered up
some part of her seems to want to imagine a future

54. *future prospects for Lebanon look bleak*
    the news announces   same announcement most days
    we're scared we won't be able to go on (Siham here)
    I saw scenes (Olivier here) *I never imagined I'd see*
    in a middle-income country   *the government's inaction*
    in the face of this unprecedented crisis   *has inflicted*
    great misery on the population   a man with diabetes
    keeps insulin in his fridge   now his insulin vials spoil
        no power to keep cool   *if prices rise how will I pay*
    (Mostafa here)   *people will die in the streets*
    that was a year ago, and people are dying in the streets
        for years the country offered us an exceptional life
    we loved it and we stayed   most nights we've been wishing
    time could stay here   so we would not have to move again

55.   again each day we have to find a way
resignation   resilience   stoicism   ignorance
way of adapting to emergency, of going daily into disaster
    & the question now, as days become longer
lighter, later, as sun begins to stretch itself to spring
concerns the wilful blindness some call determination
to be happy   and the resignation some call resilience
(or vice versa)   call it hope or call it denial
call it tiredness or call it callousness or call it intelligence
    not easy, my love, to know what to call it
all this, yes, all this, is lamentable, mysterious, all this
is out of our control   it's a relief, powerlessness
    not easy, my love, not easy   to believe in fate,
or not to believe   the question now is go on how

56. how will you cope, the emigrating(ed) diasporic
    young ask parents on the phone, on facetime, on ipads,
    trying to convince people who have lived through civil war
    and countless crises, yes, yes, lived through all this before
                go or stay, hard to tell, hard to choose
    decisions do not come easy here   decisions are not
    easy where (when) *great sadness* is, with people
    dying on the streets   not easy stay or go, not easy
    splitting families, not easy to be outside, be there
    or away split   *not easy* (Maya here) *on my father*
    to take the money but I know they need it they refuse
    to move here and we cannot go back   (George here)
    they are not poor, but they are slouching towards poverty,
    in six to seven months they might lose all their savings

57. *might lose all their savings, and then they'll be*
    dependent on me   life-savings gone now
    (Viva here) *if it wasn't for my daughter I would've left*
    a long time ago   rent generator school for my daughter
    it is not a real solution   until when are we going
    to depend on remittances   time has never
    seemed uniform, but time now is uniform as it is brazen
    time one slump, simultaneous with flagrant wrongs
    none of them   none of us   knows what to do
    no one wants to leave but we have to, to help our families
    (Ghassan here)   *the current Lebanese crisis*
    achieved what the 1982 siege of Beirut did not achieve
    the largest leading medical center in the Middle East
    was threatened with imminent collapse due to fuel shortage

58. shortage is a stuffy word on the tongue, its back end
like a block   it sounds more comic than it should
its taste is often in our mouths   our body knows it well
shortage is a reduction in what (looking back) has already
become abundance, a daily good we were accustomed
     inured   to take for granted   and war
war has become the standard of what to measure badness by
     (Bujar here) *this feels like a post-conflict situation,*
as if there had been a war two, four, or six weeks ago
(@alshykbhlalalm3 here) may God curse the government
the president of the country and every official in Lebanon
and the hospital owners   during the civil war,
which lasted about 20 years, no humiliation like this
occurred of queueing outside bakeries, power outages,

59. *power outages, fuel shortages   the lira*
    had international value   today the people
    are waiting for hours, day and night, to get bread
       war the general way we measure badness
 only its inadequacy, as measurement, as metaphor,
 is becoming plain   it comes to the fore when crises
 are different to the crisis of war   violence as potent,
 though requiring a different tool of measurement
 to cataloguing injury and counting the deceased
       Easters Catholic and Orthodox come and go
 (quietly, in hidden places, Passover too comes and goes)
 Eid al Fitr comes and goes, and makeshift temples,
 for Sikh communities, Buddhist, Sinhalese and Tamil,
 Hindu, continue their celebrations, laments, ritual

60.   ritual especially called for now
all continue their gathering of charity, knowing
they are relied on not just for hope and solace,
not just for gathering together people with shared language,
shared practice, shared vision, shared praying rhythm
    also for food, for clean and sanitised water
for guidance, spiritual and practical, for logistical
and functional aid   and they too are suffering,
which is why Ramadan is a quieter affair this year,
why iftars are not open invitations, the more the merrier,
bring your friends   why within as well as between families
there is moderation, why feasting does not quite
merit the name   as if covid were peaking again, disease
spreading again   inflation reaping what it's sown again

61. again people are heading out on boats, spreading
out their chances by getting out   they'll go first,
they tell parents partners friends children siblings,
I'll go first and let me see what it's like, I'll get money
and I'll send for you   it's got to be better than here
    refugees are going, migrant workers are going,
people without papers are going, locals are going,
like the wealthier locals who head out with visas by plane
in a mass movement of exodus nicknamed the brain drain
    many in boats go together, en famille or in groups,
and with the inflation figures for the day and the value
of the lira to the dollar for the day and the reports on protest
movements for the day, the news also features, less regularly
and less prominently, the numbers on failed boats today

62. today, we are discovering, our body is discovering,
today is likely to surprise us   it's so likely to surprise us
the surprise won't be strange, it won't astonish, won't
seize us in the gut   even the reports of people
leaving people they hired to help them at home
    leaving people on the street outside embassy doors
because, thanks to the plummeting of the lira, they
can't afford to pay the dollars of their wages   even
these reports of abandonment meet with nods of acceptance
    abandonment is a common consequence these days,
two and a half years in   even while people
(so many people)   help each other   the odd thing is
neither abandonment nor help any longer have power
to surprise   two and a half years in

63. in May (the news announces) transport costs
    increased 515 percent   health sector costs
    increased 468 percent   water, electricity, gas, fuels
    increased 445 percent   food & nonalcoholic drinks
    increased 364 percent   inflation is not close
    to its peak, 741 percent in 1987   but this shows
    only that there is still a way to go
            when last they met on the dusklit path,
    enjoying the new-sprung taste of summering heat,
    the man said, it's not as bad as the war
    because most days this is what his father says   it's not
    as bad as the war   it's when we begin to say, yes,
    this is as bad as war   well then fear
        fear might overwhelm the will to go on

64. on we go and *we should have stopped by now!*
is something someone says daily
resilience is not a thing to praise people for
resilience is not an individual quality   it is a condition
made possible by other conditions   it is a property
belonging to material and immaterial structures   it is
a thing to weigh up in your hand when taking the measure
of a fabric   *we are no longer able to bear the situation*
(company statement here)   *we thought for a while*
we would be able to overcome, armed with a sense
of professionalism and national responsibility, but
   we were in front of a dead end
       (Nasser here)   *everything*
that happened   *could've been avoidable*

65. avoidable, let's be honest, is not any longer
a word we understand, not avoidable, not inevitable
time has shifted into something that does not move
inexorably towards a single throbbing goal   there is
nothing we are heading towards and therefore
have to collide with or escape from   instead time is
absolutely haphazard   anything could happen
at any time   we've accepted everything, even explosions
on the border of the sea, even a fire burning away bodies
who were here until now   we've begun to normalise
& we've begun to know the danger of normalising
we're accustomed (inured) to a ground shifting beneath our feet
our body no longer anticipates safety, no longer anticipates
anything but stopping   as time   twists into something geologic

66. geologic calls to tectonic, calls to earth, calls to body
body turning ways it would not turn in another climate
another geography another space   body turning
into what body does not recognise, would not recognise
outside or beyond the context, the conditions,
the unthought eerie structures, making body this way
making body work and not work this way   these days
people are going to the beach   it's one way to pass time
      when the woman and the man meet for a walk
after two months of being too busy or too heavy
to manage the effort   they say nice things to each other
about appearances, though (he thinks) she looks old, though
(she thinks) he looks bloated, and though (each thinks)
the other looks less urgent and less ardent than they did

67. did you hear the latest, she says, about the strikes
    I wish them luck, he says, what else is there to do,
but stop things going on the way we're used to them going on
    my cousin, she says, every time I see him, my cousin
says *hit us, we're ready!* he knows we've got to swallow
a painful pill, but he thinks the sooner the better, and then
at least we'll turn around, instead of rotting here in this same
fetid mush   how's your sleep, she asks, when he
doesn't respond   because suddenly she's thinking, maybe
maybe he's already so hit   the idea of another smash
across the face, in the belly, wham straight into the crotch,
maybe a blow to the body   will fell him, while her family
    her family will stagger, and gather, and stand
        my sleep's fine, he says

68. say you want to say something very unlikely, almost
    magical in the way it happens, or the timing of it,
    the sheer collision of coincidence, the serendipity
    say you want to show up contrast between a then-and-now
    you'd try to see how things were on one day, then examine
    the following year   you'd make your own anniversary
        two years after the port explosion, to the day
    though not to the minute, nor to the hour, but
    precisely two years   one of the silos collapses
            as if the structures themselves were keeping time
    as if they   like the rest of us   thought two years
    was really a time that ought to be marked, given
    the respect of a nod, and, realising the lack of such a gesture,
    made a mark of their own   took a stand   fell

69. *fell, and the rest will fall over soon* (Samer here)
   they should too they're only a symbol of failure
   two weeks later 350 judges go on strike   *what activity
   is there still in a country full of collapse   we have been
   working in deplorable conditions for years, without electricity,
   without equipment, invaded by waste no one picks up anymore
      our salaries no longer allow us to pay the price of gasoline
   to get to the courthouse*   the information ministry
   goes on strike   an anonymous source, an employee,
   says salaries barely cover transport costs   men
   (it's mostly men) spend hours queuing for state-subsidised
   bread available on the black market at four times the price
      let them open the door to emigration so we can leave
   (Khaled here)   *we can't live in our country*

70. countrywide, new fuel prices are proclaimed
     midsummer now, and the newspaper announces
new fuel prices   20 liters of 95 & 98 octane gasoline
increased by 3,000   reaching 572,000 and 584,000
respectively   the cost of 20 liters of diesel remained
the same at 663,000   the cost of a cylinder of household gas
also remained the same at 321,000
    next morning, a new declaration
new fuel prices   20 liters of 95 & 98 octane gasoline
increased by 3,000 and 4,000 respectively, reaching
575,000 and 588,000   the cost of 20 liters of diesel
increased by 27,000, reaching 690,000   the cost
of a cylinder of household gas increased by 7,000,
reaching 328,000   *we can't live in our country*

71. *country!* the woman and her friends have been laughing
when they hear this word used to describe their land
all day long people complain about *this country*
this goddamn mess of a country and they've begun to say,
in reply, call this a country!   it invariably provokes
a smile a joke a curse   an emoji of steaming poo
or gif of a drowning man   a lightbulb with no electricity
a picture of a candle, which has come to symbolise
the newfound luxury of this middle-income state,
which prided itself on being playground of the middle east,
gateway to arabia, to europe   in parliament (a newspaper reports)
there is no fuel to run a generator for the elevator, so security guards
run messages up and down stairs   a public servant's
monthly wage has dropped from $1000 to fifty, and counting

72. counting, the painful unceasing activity of the moment
soldiers' salaries are so low they are taking on second
and third jobs, despite the prohibition against it
if you go to register a new car   (if you do, we will ask
how and with what foreign money you bought it)
you will be given a handwritten note instead of state-issued
documents, because of the shortage of paper   (Faisal here)
the judges are hungry   (Walid here) *our lives
have become primitive*   nearly 6/10 in the public sector
plan to leave, a pace equivalent to the exodus of war
    these are people we need for recovery (Lamia here)
       the past years destroyed all our efforts (Walid here)
        the question is what will be left
         and also how will this end

73. end is surely a fantastic word, there is only what goes on
and what it turns into as it continues going on, there are
not starts and stops, ends and finishes, final flourishes
    this is a truth we've learnt since the port explosion
and others learn it in their devastations, their deaths & griefs,
their moments of eye-to-eye recognition, which are
never quite acknowledged by the world beyond   the sky
does not fall, and if it darkens, it is only because
it is covered temporarily by smoke and sorrow   the sky
will lift the sun will emerge the scent of new life
will expand and flower   and memorials
will be forgotten unless they are tended to
    on some days there was more war than others
    the war ended early and it hasn't ended at all

74. already one year since the August-born child
    came from the womb through the birth canal
    through warm wet flesh, through damp hair, came
    slobbery in all the body's mess, came crying   first
    a little tentatively, till the feeling of creating sound
    was familiar all through the body, and the mews grew
    to yawling grew to bawls   came crying & sleeping
    into the world   one year since the man from the mountains
    held small slippery flesh, flesh of his own body,
    bones built from his own blood, his own love,
    his nervous system and his choices   body born
    of his and his wife's body   one year   and
    the things they thought   the things we thought   might be
    different   well, both nothing and everything have changed

75. change is a slippery thing, an uncertain sliding thing
    change is white and heavy, like furniture falling from the sky
    straight towards your face, not even inescapable because
    it's on you before the concept of escape has become possible
        change is sultry, flickering, familiar, insinuating itself
    before you realise what is really on the cards it holds   flagrantly
    fragrantly, sweeping mysteriously   before your face
        the only consistent thing of change is   your face
    is transformed by it before you understand it is there
    change might be a heavy mask, down over your nostrils,
    making breathing thin, stippling air, stopping up light
    might be barbs in your skin   might be touch of gentle water
        change is what we call for   it is both
    too much change and not enough change we mourn for

76. four young boys have taken to playing on the path
    where we gather to meet, where those whose bodies
    bounce and flutter can run, plug their music
    into ears and pull sunglasses down onto noses
    and run, run, run through air and wind, run through
    thick summer air, till sweat, accumulating on skin,
    pools and trembles down deep down, limbs to ground,
    to tarmac and earth, or is flecked off foreheads, streaming
    in hair   & the way the woman walked with the man, up a hill,
    is a way intrepid runners go, and so it's often quiet
    and at its peak, four young boys, two sets of brothers,
    whose families live in the parking-lots of the big houses,
    spend their days together, they're there from nine till six,
    running into the shaded parking where their moms are

77. where their moms are keeping rooms clean,
    where their moms are cooking and talking
    with other women who are home all day, while men,
    men keep away even if they don't have work to do
    because to see them sitting around in daytime makes
    everyone miserable   makes everyone miserable
    and confuses the kids, who assume it's a feast day
    and wonder what happened to make the feast days,
    which once seemed so brief, burgeon like this in daily life
        the boys run in when it gets too hot, they have lunch,
    they have spoons of what was or will be lunch as snacks,
            mostly they are outside playing
    there's enough shade beneath the trees, and summer
    is too fun to waste waiting for weather to cool

78.   cool down with water, except now water
is rarely cold when it comes from the fridge,
it's warm, because the fridge is mostly a cupboard
it runs only if electricity does   and though
the building has a generator these families do not benefit,
not since they too were called on to pay the subscription
following a vote from the building committee, despite
the fact a home comes, supposedly, with the job
of looking after the place   simpler, then, to keep away
from the generator, unless on someone else's behalf,
and so the fridge whirs its work for a small segment of the day,
and, for the rest, the women cook as they go, men buy
as they go   it's more expensive & more inefficient
& more time-wasting that way   at least the boys like to play

79. play together under the sun   they like the way
this path up a hill is private to them, mostly,
except most days, for the last six weeks or more
(the boys aren't counting, they're aged five and four)
there's been a disruption in the form of a runner
a woman who catches their eye because her hair is light
and her legs and arms gleam in the sun, and they've
taken to shouting to her, hi, hi, when she's on her way
up the hill, and she shouts it back, hi, hi, hi, hi!
over and over again, as if the word is all that's needed
for conversation, as if new information is imparted
with every repetition, and after weeks on end of this
it's part of the boys' routine, they look out for a runner
and when she comes they stand as to salute   hi, hi, hi

80. hi, hi-iii   they've learnt to waver their voices
    on the word, same as she does, and the youngest of them
    does it for as long as his breath will hold, hi-iiiiiiiiiiiiiii
    the word familiar to his tongue as ekol or nom or kahraba
         they decide they'd like to give her something
    they tell their mothers, and the women laugh at the game
    ! give a gift to the runner !   let's invite her for coffee,
    one mom suggests, but the boys veto this
          too adult, too boring, too bitter a taste
    and the runner is their personal plaything, she appears
    from nowhere and shouts to them   to have her sitting
    inside with their moms over ahweh would be a move
    they don't like the look of   but giving her a gift
    the smile and surprise of it   this they can & will do

81. doing their best not to give it away when she comes
 — they can't get the words out, there's too much
 to think about, they've got to approach her
 while she's running, and what if she doesn't stop —
     it's the two eldest, the five-year-olds, who take
 on the task, and when they see her begin her slog along
 the hill (they know they must catch her on the way up
 when the going is slow and she seems more likely
 to distract either them or herself with yodelling *hiiiiiii*)
 they pick up their gift and move closer to the path
 and they call look, look, stop, look   the runner stops
     the first time the meeting between them has held tempo
 like this, instead of being in motion   the boys are confused
 and she is red   they hold out a big pack of tissues

82. a big pack of tissues, not pocket size   the kind
you stuff in a holder, the kind that could come in a box,
only pliable plastic is better able to go in the holder,
and it's cheaper too   the runner's raw face
seems strange close up   the boys thrust the packet
towards her, shouting gift, here take it! for you!
and the feeling when it's in her hands and not in theirs,
when normality is back, brings such relief to their body
their voices get stronger   their voices shout
hi, hi, hi, hi, hi-iiiii   with a vigour they've not yet had
and the younger two join in, till cacophony has replaced
ceremonial gift-giving, and the runner's repeated thanks
are safely obliterated in the daily ritual of salutation
    the boys have honoured the conversation

83. conversation is both more honest and less, these days
　　　　　hardship is widespread enough
　　that the shame of admission is not what it would be
　　were it not for the structural nature of catastrophe
　　　　　but still　　we tend to talk about the situation
　　　　　rather than　　what our body is getting used to
　　　　　　　　　　what our land is getting used to
　　all the workers are on strike and no one has fixed anything
　　(no name here)
　　at the beginning of September the news announces
　　20 liters of 95-gas increased by 12,000　　reaching 628,000
　　20 liters of 98-gas increased by 13,000　　reaching 643,000
　　　　(Nasser here)　　*it's all kicking the can down the road*
　　　　　　　　　　　　　　　　it's true

84. it's true   we are all at sea   except
every day people really are at sea, taking to water to find
a better life   which is nothing other than to find
a place where the same life can move differently
    with 95% of the lira's value gone, one paper
begins a series asking, but how are the Lebanese managing
    here men are angry, where (when) no money is
where (when) hunger is, where aimlessness and joblessness is,
where time hangs heavy and what is urgent is relieving
the build-up of a body's particular physical anguish
there is an increase in femicide   there is an increase
in attempts to put an end to one's days   there is an increase
in violence against women, in particular at home, in particular
against young women, young wives   this summer

85. this summer Hanaa is burnt alive   twelve days later she dies
Ghinwa is beaten by her husband, who films as he goes
Nabila is left by her husband in hospital following her death
he flees immediately after   it's another way disaster
has become a daily thing   & though we have come to nod,
accept the arrival of bad news, we know nodding along
is a kind of self-protection   it does not lessen despair
    bolstering against shock   it's a grace, perhaps, to be
surprised   (Leila here)   *women are first to pay the price
in this time of crisis   violence is exacerbated and women
are the weak link*   women are the first port-of-call
laws for women's protection exist (Ghida here) *unfortunately
the collapse of the state and the consequent lack of means
do not make our task easier*   (Wlek here) *all my prayers*

86. *prayers for the rest of these souls   of these true martyrs
of humanity   and may the appropriate punishment
for their torturers be immediate   the torturers are
the men in question   behind them is the non-existent state
(Bassma here) find me a way out of here and I will take it*
an armed gang kills a money exchanger and badly injures
another without getting any cash   *we've arrived* (Nizar here)
*in a moment where even those who have money can't procure
milk for their babies*   (Rima here) *I was passing my time
in the car looking for boxes of formula for my son   I went
to Tripoli, Saida*   Rima sold her gold to buy a box of milk
I have nothing left to sell   (Souheil here) *parents
are telling me they're replacing formula with water and anise,
or sugar, or even with milk for three-year-olds   it's terrible*

87. *it's terrible   what is happening is unacceptable*
(Faisal here) *this is definitely a failed state*   ministers say
the lack of stock could have various causes   could be
stockpiling by parents frightened by successive shortages
could be pharmacies wanting to make a profit   could be
for the purpose of smuggling   *the ministry is surprised
by the shortage of infant milk reported on the market, and regrets,
at this difficult stage, the lack of solidarity and responsibility*
(yes, we too think the use of these words undermines
their chance for meaning)   meanwhile, on the coast
a boat is returned   at least 60 people started out on it
Lebanese, Palestinians, Syrians   nowadays this is called
irregular migration   these people went (Abou here)
    to seek a decent life for themselves and their families

88. families the reason why   hope the reason why
         a few months earlier one of these boats sank
     11 bodies were found   a report says the number of people
     who tried to leave Lebanon by sea nearly doubled in 2021
     from 2020   the figure rose again by more than 70%
     in 2022   *no one gets on these death boats lightly* (Philippe here)
     people are taking this perilous decision, risking their lives
     in search of dignity   dignity, in this as in every case,
     means being able to envision a future, means believing
     what you're building is solid   at least has a chance
     to be solid   the future you imagine does not need even
     to be likely   it needs only to be possible to project
     and beneath that   it needs to be possible to dream
          (Barbara here)   *we do what we can with each day*

89. days have begun to merge together   same as talk
    on and off the street   we notice patterns, currents,
    tendencies, repetitions, cycles   *a beggar extends his hand*
    forward, a cab driver asks for alms by stretching it backward
    (Tarek here)   we notice mirrors, reminders, likenesses
    notice a protest movement in one city echoed by parallel action
    in another   and now   as before   as always
         people are taking matters into their own hands
    Bassam holds up the Federal Bank in Hamra, rifle in fist,
    saying he will set himself on fire if not permitted to withdraw
    his savings to pay for his father's medical treatment
    a crowd supports him, chanting *down with the rules of the banks*
    social media watches   people on streets & in offices are proud
    the action he is taking is an action   social media watches

90. social media watches   society, through its media,
    shouts encouragement   charges against Bassam
    are dropped, and he gets some, though not all, not half
    or a quarter, of his money   his name becomes a hashtag
            hope   resistance   change
    a month later Sali takes a toy gun, borrowed from her nephew,
    heads to Blom Bank in Sodeco, saying she wants her money
    for her sister's cancer treatment   she's part of an activist group,
    staking a claim for a people's cause through a single case
         in Halba activists burn tyres in the road
    two days later, five more attacks by depositors on banks
         the banks say they will take *any measures necessary*
    for the safety of employees   while, on the street, people
    are beaten for demonstrating for the release of two activists

91. demonstrating for the release of two activists, these days,
even if coordinated, planned, timed, thought-out,
is risky business   *they hit me in the head, in the shoulder*
(Ali here) *they started to threaten us   every time I spoke*
they got annoyed and beat me more   Bassam, like Abdallah,
like Mohammed, went free, but times have already changed,
and *vigilante withdrawals* become à la mode, with army veterans
& MPs getting in on the act, bringing the number of holdups
in one week to six, with threats for bank-owners' houses
to be burnt down too   and now the association of banks declares
all banks throughout the country will close indefinitely
    yes, despite the rapid pace of change, this is all
one long day   everything that happens is already the same
every time I spoke they got annoyed and beat me more

92. more stats are released   as we try to come to terms
           try to get a grip   try to maintain some purchase
    try to grasp   just what is going on here
    over the last school year some students at some schools
    — yes, the state-run schools — had 50 days of classes
         a shelter for children of very poor families
    who cannot afford to keep them — could not afford them
    before any of this began — their intake of children
    doubles in a year   a research centre releases a report
    putting the average teacher's monthly income at $131
    their monthly commute at $128   92% of parents
    struggle to pay their children's journey to school
         the public sector (Chaar here)
    the public sector is at its end if we keep going like this

93.   this is all one long day
           we are in a state of collapse (Lamia here)
     this is the realm of anguish where parents are unable
     to buy for their children   children unable to pay
     for parents' care   families and friends unable
     to look after each other, use their means to care for each other
     anguish of families unable to save, unable to earn, unable to project
     kids stay kids in the eyes of parents   and of themselves
     this is all one long day   (Michel here) *the money will run out*
            what can we say   money   money   money
     (Chaar here) *no state employee is able to buy a kilo*
     of meat or chicken except maybe once a month
                we are only buying basic necessities
                     this is all one long day

94. days now where basics are the cost of luxuries
    84% of households do not have money for necessities
    70% have to borrow money for food or buy food on credit
        credit itself in trouble now
    (Chaar here) *the past years destroyed all our efforts*
        a report is released with a father saying
    my son does not trust me anymore and does not call me baba,
    because I am not fulfilling my role as a father
    days where fuel prices fluctuate on the market like cash
        sometimes there is a small decrease
    but mostly the trend continues   up   up   up
    and as October begins (marking, if you please, *three years*
    since this began) 20 liters of 95-gasoline   is 710,000
    a kiloliter of generator fuel is $980.56 $23 up from last

95. last year or month or week is a pointless comparison-point
        there is only these days   and these are days
  when it's getting cold again   another cycle beginning again
  I'm relying on God now (Tarek here) *God will not let me down*
     organisations are collecting data collecting stats
there are so many NGOs that asked for ways to help me
they took so much information and wasted so much of my time
but no one got back to me with any help (unnamed boy here)
    I no longer have even spare change (Nour here)
but at least my son is American
         yes, this is all one long day
but what something else looks like
is an act of imagination   one has to have lived
          not too many one-long-days to be able to see

96. see how the woman follows the way of the weather
    she comes down from the mountains where her teta
    has a house   she spent the summer there after her work
    said they'd have to stop renting the office and work
    would go remote   now the mountain is set to turn cold
    and she's back in town, down for winter and reality,
    away from lush land, where grapes malfouf tomatoes grow,
    where she walks to see goat-babies and sheep-babies,
    where she can pet them, if she's quiet and a little slow,
    where reality is softer, away from queues and car-horns,
    away from constant swapping of news, where she and teta
    play backgammon and sometimes chess, where,
    in days of childish summer, she was given
    her own small patch of garden for zaatar and ba'adounis

97. zaatar and ba'adounis with her now, freshly snipped
    from the mountain where she first walked her way alone
    down to the village to fetch yoghurt fresh from goats
        this summer she spent her days on the computer
    trying to encourage teta to tell stories of the past
    instead of alternating between asking & telling her
            about what's happening now
    it was covid, teta said, which was the really bad thing
        the only time she knows teta is worried is when teta
    asks how she will cope, with her wrong-currency-salary
    and still-bare-finger, or when teta remarks their only wealth
    is in the family's house, dropping in value as time goes on
            it won't in any case help with daily price-rises
            won't help even if they sell now

98. now she's back in her town above the city, her surest
hotplot of home, a place her friends come calling,
her sisters lie about sprawling, her brother mocks
and watches out for her, and she mocks him for trying
to defend her, a place where all of them, all along the road,
all those who've been here years, all of them watch
for each other   you know those boys, her brother says,
the ones who play along the way   this summer
they gave Lana tissues for a gift   let's take them something
clothes or games and toys   she nods okay,
knowing he wants her to do it   yesterday teta
asked what way is there out of this   teta asked
as if discussion could come up with an answer
        if there is to be an answer   perhaps it will come after

99. after a few days, carrying bonbons for the boys,
    she meets the man along the path   she is dressed
    for the weather, and his hair is most definitely oiled
    she wonders if beneath his shirt the cross she glimpsed
    in summer sits   wonders whether he has hair there
    wonders whether to ask him how he's doing, or keep
    conversation light   light falls by early evening now,
    after half an hour they are in darkness
        wind feels strong, and they walk, at his request,
    back towards a lamppost, where they stand,
    she pulling a little on her sleeves   it could be
    this place is a contaminated landscape   could be
    it will always return to what it knows, and what it knows
    has most potently been war   war and migration

100. migration   more than 100 people who left Lebanon
by boat in September have been recovered drowned
    there are 21 survivors, with around 30 still missing
the boat capsized off the coast of Tartus   boats
still leaving   people still going   while she and he
stand by a lamppost with too many wires dangling from it
and who knows how long the light will last for
    both of them were late, delayed by fuel queues
    it would be funny if the queues weren't so normal
a better excuse, nowadays, than the old traffic complaints
too quick to trip off the tongue   do you like looking up,
he says, and she realises she's watching electric wires
slash across the sky, silhouetted against dusk by lamplight
    I was just   smell the pines, he says

101. says nothing more, and she inhales the same cloying needles
every nose of here smells, and though this forest was burnt,
though it's a quarter of the size it was when she was a girl,
though these bushes and gorse-plants, these thistles and clay-soils,
though these pines were burnt, the land is here
I tell the people change has to come, even if myself I don't believe
cases now of cholera, and she does not know what will come
      her body and the body of her country is already written on,
her body, her family's, the body of this man she knows
and does not know who stands beside her, this body
who does nothing other than sleep, work, bed   or her body
who sits, smokes, eats, waits, like the body of her land,
waiting daily amidst disaster   *three years since this began*
they will walk, give the boys bonbons, then inshallah sleep

NOTES ON ARABIC WORDS

1. nom, cheghel, takhet: sleep, work, bed

3. schwe schwe: little by little

12. raqwe: pan for boiling coffee

17 & 101. inshallah: God willing

21. moloukhiye: meal of chicken, rice, and spinach

26. ayre bi hazze: my penis in my luck – idiom approximate to 'fuck my luck'

26. kahraba: electricity

37 & 38. haram: something offensive to God – used formally and colloquially

37. mish haram: isn't that haram
    mballa haram: yes, it is haram

51. loz akhdar: green almonds

80. ekol or nom or kahraba: food or sleep or electricity
    ahweh: coffee

96. teta: grandma
    malfouf: cabbage
    zaatar and ba'adounis: thyme and parsley

LAY OUT YOUR UNREST

www.ingramcontent.com/pod-product-compliance
Lightning Source LLC
Chambersburg PA
CBHW070049100426
42734CB00040B/2887